Origins
Big Game Adventure

Alison Hawes ■ Jorge Santillan

OXFORD
UNIVERSITY PRESS

Mission impossible?

Dr Richard Jones is sitting at his computer in the offices of *Animals in Danger*, looking worried.

"What is it, Dad?" asks Mark.

"It's this email," says Richard. "It's the third request for help I've had today."

"So what are you going to do?"

"I'm not sure we can *do* anything," says Richard. "If it wasn't for this," he says, tapping the plaster on his leg, "Liam and I could go."

Liam is Mark's older brother. He has been on lots of expeditions to help animals that have been in danger. But Richard has a strict rule that no one ever goes on a mission on their own. In fact, Richard has written a book called *Animals in Danger Safety Handbook*.

"Something does have to be done ASAP," says Richard, "or it will be too late."

"You could always send me!" Mark says, half joking, half hoping.

"That's not such a bad idea," Liam replies, coming into the room. "I could teach Mark how to stay safe and help the animals at the same time."

Richard looks unconvinced.

"Come on, Dad," urges Liam, "I'm eighteen.

I've led loads of missions. You know I'll look after Mark."

"I know," says Richard, "but …"

"Please, Dad," begs Mark.

"If we don't go, who will?" says Liam.

Mark holds his breath.

"OK," Richard says at last. "But make sure Mark stays with you *at all times* and that he reads that book of mine before he goes!"

"Thanks, Dad!" Mark grins. "I won't let you down."

Richard hands Liam some files. "These are your missions," he says.

SELECT MISSION

Mark and Liam have three missions to carry out. Select the first mission you would like to go on with them.

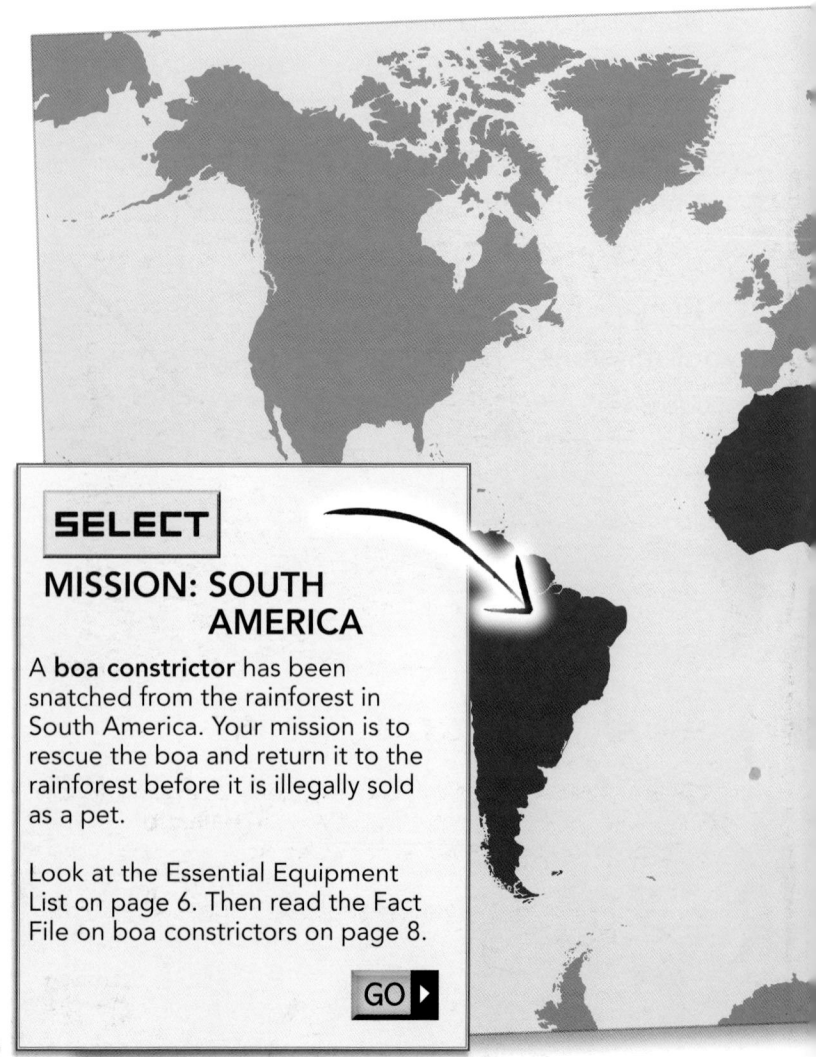

SELECT

MISSION: SOUTH AMERICA

A **boa constrictor** has been snatched from the rainforest in South America. Your mission is to rescue the boa and return it to the rainforest before it is illegally sold as a pet.

Look at the Essential Equipment List on page 6. Then read the Fact File on boa constrictors on page 8.

GO ▶

SELECT | MISSION: ASIA

A **tiger** has wandered out of its reserve onto nearby farmland. The farmers are worried the tiger may attack them or their animals. Your mission is to find the tiger and return it to the reserve, before anyone gets hurt.

Look at the Essential Equipment List on page 6. Then read the Fact File on tigers on page 9.

GO ▶

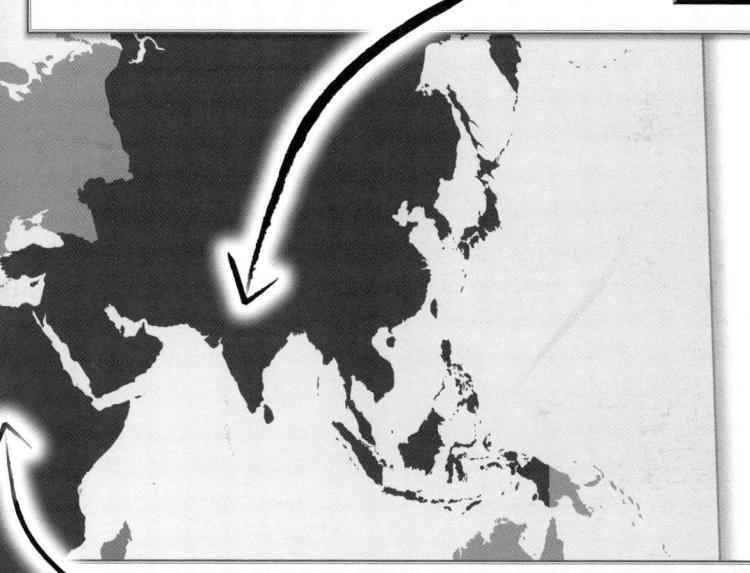

SELECT | MISSION: AFRICA

A **black rhino** has been trapped by poachers in the African bush. Your mission is to set the rhino free before the poachers return to kill it and sell its horns.

Look at the Essential Equipment List on page 6. Then read the Fact File on page 7.

GO ▶

ESSENTIAL EQUIPMENT LIST

Mark tries to read the *Animals in Danger Safety Handbook* before he leaves, but he is so excited he can't concentrate. He thinks about taking the book with him, but it is far too heavy to pack. And anyway, he tells himself, he isn't likely to get into any trouble with Liam to look after him …

Fact File: RHINOCEROS

General: There are five species of rhinoceros. Some species have two horns and others have one.

Population: There are about 3700 black rhinos left in the wild.

Status: ENDANGERED

Threats: Poachers

Diet: Grass and leaves

Live: Parts of Africa and Asia

Behaviour: Rhinos usually live alone. They use their horns to defend themselves.

Did you know?
Rhinos are one of the most endangered animals on Earth.

Start Mission

▶ Turn to page 10 to start Mission: Africa ◀

Fact File: BOA CONSTRICTOR

General: Boa constrictors are large snakes. The largest boa ever found was more than 5 metres long.

Status: Some boas are ENDANGERED. Many are PROTECTED.

Threats: Poachers and loss of habitat

Diet: Birds and small animals

Live: Mainly found in South and Central America.

Behaviour: Boas kill their prey by squeezing it until it can no longer breathe.

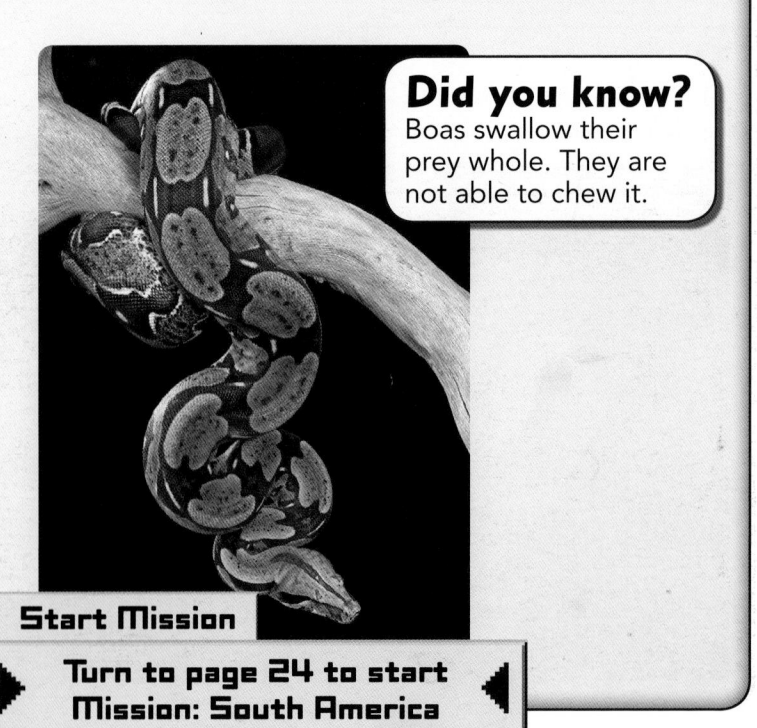

Did you know?
Boas swallow their prey whole. They are not able to chew it.

Start Mission
▶ Turn to page 24 to start Mission: South America ◀

Fact File: TIGER

General: Tigers are the largest members of the cat family.

Population: About 3000 to 4500 tigers exist in the wild today.

Status: ENDANGERED

Threats: Poachers and loss of habitat

Diet: Mostly deer and water buffalo

Live: Parts of Asia

Behaviour: Tigers ambush their prey and kill it with a bite to the neck.

Did you know?
Tigers are very good swimmers.

Start Mission

◀ Turn to page 38 to start Mission: Asia ▶

MISSION: AFRICA

Your mission is to release the black rhino.
To reach the rhino, there are two possible paths to follow:

Start 1

▶ **To start at the rock formation, turn to page 12.** ◀

Start 2

▶ **To start at the baobab tree, turn to page 18.** ◀

Start 1 | Mission: Africa

Liam and Mark climb up onto a rock and study the map. From here they can see for miles across the scrub and grassland. Liam shields his eyes and looks up at the sky. Dark clouds are gathering across the sun. The wind has begun to pick up, but the air is still very hot. Mark takes a long drink from his water bottle. Even the water tastes hot. Across the grassland, the animals have noticed the change in the weather, too. Herds of wildebeest and zebra mill around in the distance.

Liam points to the map. Apart from a few solitary trees, the forest that they are heading for is the only real cover for miles. Liam jumps down from the rock.

"There's bad weather on the way," he says. "We'd better get going. We don't want to be out in the open when the storm hits."

Liam moves off at a brisk pace. Mark has to run to keep up. Every now and then a flash of lightning lights up the sky. Mark counts the seconds until he hears the rumble of thunder that follows the lightning.

"It's getting closer," he says, as a massive clap of thunder sounds overhead.

Mark spots a giant cloud coming towards them.

"A dust storm!" he warns.

"I think it might be a stampede," says Liam. As the cloud of dust gets closer, Mark can see that Liam is right. Spooked by the storm, a herd of wild-eyed elephants is charging towards them.

The nearest clump of trees is fifty metres away. It is their only hope. Mark seems rooted to the spot. Liam half drags, half pushes him, through the dry grass. In the end, there is no time to climb a tree. They flatten themselves against a tree trunk and hold on tight, as the herd thunders by.

"Thanks," says Mark, when the elephants have gone. "That was terrifying! I had no idea what to do."

"You really must read Dad's book!" says Liam.

It starts to rain. They make a run for the forest. Here, at last, they slow their pace – partly to catch their breath, partly because the path up ahead is uphill and narrow. As the path narrows, it gradually becomes more and more overgrown. They have to use their hiking poles to beat a path through the dense foliage. It is hard work and after an hour or so they stop for a rest and something to eat.

They are just getting some food out of their backpacks when, suddenly, large shapes crash through the jungle towards them. There are thumping and screaming sounds and the noise of branches being torn apart. Mark feels his heart turn over with fear.

"What is it? he asks.

"It's a troop of baboons!" says Liam. "Quick, hide behind a bush and keep quiet," he whispers.

But Mark doesn't hear him. He is already running back the way they have come. When he looks back it isn't Liam that is behind him – he's face to face with a male baboon baring its teeth ...!

GAME OVER! THE BABOON HAS GOT YOU!

Start 2

▶ Turn to page 18 to restart your mission at the baobab tree. ◀

Survival Tip

▶ To find out how to survive an encounter with a baboon, read the extract from *Animals in Danger Safety Handbook* on page 54. ◀

New Mission

▶ To select a new mission, turn to pages 4–5. ◀

Start 2 | Mission: Africa

Liam and Mark are standing under a giant baobab tree. The air is thick with heat. Lightning is sparking in the distant sky.

"We'd better get going," says Liam. "We don't want to be here if the storm comes this way."

As they set off through the long grass, keeping themselves low to the ground, lightning flashes ever closer.

Minutes later, there is an enormous crash as a huge fork of lightning hits the baobab tree, causing it to burst into flames.

They stare in horror as a branch falls on the bone dry grass and sets it alight. The fire quickly spreads to within metres of where they are standing.

"Go!" screams Liam.

They run for their lives towards the river. The flames are spreading almost as fast as they can run, burning everything in their path. The thick smoke leaves them gasping for air.

Quickly, they pull a clean shirt and a water bottle from their backpacks. Soaking the shirts with water, they each hold them over their mouth and nose as they run. Five minutes later, with the flames licking at their heels, they reach the river and wade in.

On the other side, they stop to catch their breath and drink what is left of their water. Smoke is still billowing towards them, but the river stops the fire going any further.

Liam quickly checks the map. The forest where the rhino is being held is up ahead.

Slowly they walk into the forest. They hear the rhino before they see it.

Alarmed by the smell of smoke, the rhino is doing all it can to escape. It repeatedly charges at the metal fence that surrounds it. But the fence holds fast under the rhino's enormous weight.

There is a gate on one side of the fence. Liam and Mark only have to pull back the bolt and the rhino will be free. But it isn't going to be quite that simple. As Liam points out, a frightened, cornered rhino is one of the most dangerous creatures on earth.

Then he has an idea. "We could put a rope around the bolt and open the gate from the safety of that tree over there," he says, pointing towards a tree a little way away.

They knot their ropes together and Liam ties one end to the bolt. But as they walk to the tree, they realize the rope isn't going to be long enough. Liam isn't sure what to do next.

Mark reaches for his backpack. He has an idea, too.

Mark pulls out all his spare clothes, knots them together and ties them to the end of the rope.

"Brilliant!" says Liam.

As they climb the tree, they find the rope is now the right length. Mark counts to three. They pull hard on the rope. The bolt shoots back with a loud crack. The gate swings open and the rhino gallops to freedom in a cloud of dust.

"Now, all we have to do is alert the local police that there are poachers in the area," says Liam, "and our job here is done."

"Mission accomplished!" says Mark.

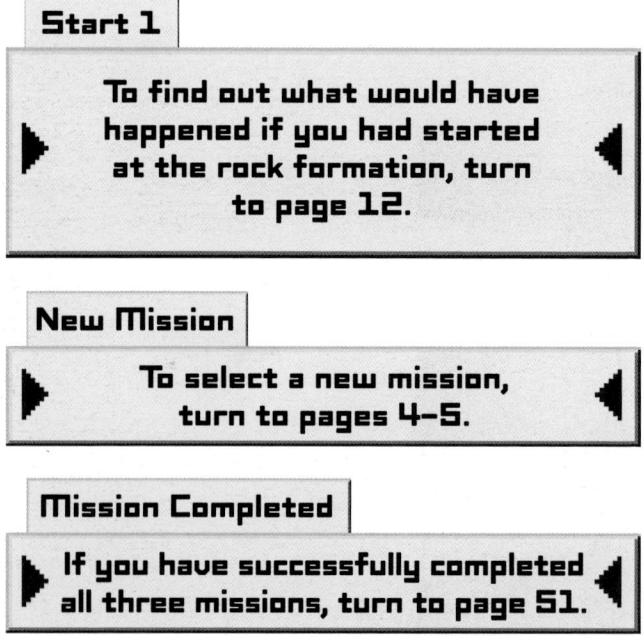

Start 1

▶ To find out what would have happened if you had started at the rock formation, turn to page 12. ◀

New Mission

▶ To select a new mission, turn to pages 4–5. ◀

Mission Completed

▶ If you have successfully completed all three missions, turn to page 51. ◀

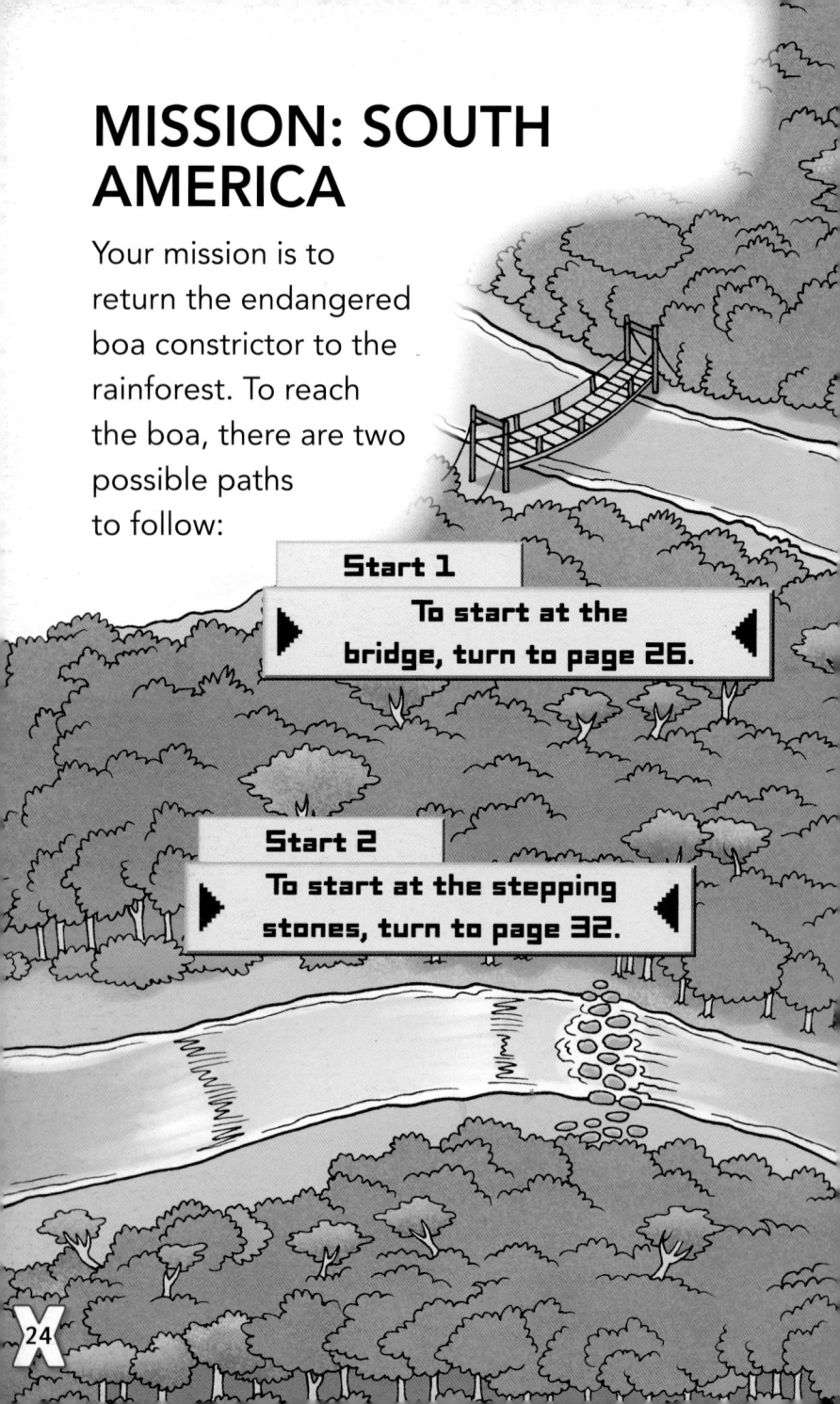

MISSION: SOUTH AMERICA

Your mission is to return the endangered boa constrictor to the rainforest. To reach the boa, there are two possible paths to follow:

Start 1

▶ **To start at the bridge, turn to page 26.** ◀

Start 2

▶ **To start at the stepping stones, turn to page 32.** ◀

Start 1 | Mission: South America

Mark doesn't like the way the bridge moves as they walk across it.

"Bridges like this always sway a bit," says Liam. Mark grabs at the rope rails to steady himself but that only makes things worse.

Halfway across, a piece of timber snaps as Liam steps on it.

"Watch out!" yells Mark, as one of Liam's feet disappears through a hole in the bridge floor.

As Liam pulls his foot out, one of the rope rails snaps. The bridge lurches violently and hangs at an angle. Mark screams and clings to what is left of the bridge.

Far below, the river runs fast and deep.

"We're going to have to jump!" Liam yells, pulling off his backpack and dropping it into the river.

"I can't!" shouts Mark, as his backpack hits the water.

"We've no choice," says Liam. "Now listen to me. Feet together, arms down. Now ... jump!"

Mark takes a deep breath and concentrates on keeping his body straight as he hits the water. When he bobs back to the surface, he grabs his backpack and holds on to it like a float.

The current pulls him downstream. Liam is nowhere to be seen.

Washed up on the river bank, Mark staggers out of the water. He needs to rest but he can't – not until he knows Liam is safe.

He climbs a tree to get a better view of the river. He is relieved to see his brother walking towards him. Liam is soaking wet and has lost his backpack but apart from that he looks fine.

They sit in the sun and eat the dried meat and fruit that Mark has in his backpack, while their clothes dry out.

Once they have recovered, they check the map, which Mark has been carrying in his backpack. As the river has washed them up downstream, they have further to walk to get to the hut they are looking for. They set off.

After a while they find the hut, hidden in the forest. It is empty except for a large glass tank. The boa constrictor is coiled up in one corner of it.

"I'm not sure what to do now," says Liam. "I was going to use my hiking pole to lift the boa out of the tank but I've lost it along with everything else."

"I've lost mine too," says Mark, "but I've got another idea." He looks in his backpack. He has a spare T-shirt, a whistle, a bottle of water and some rope.

They wash their hands with the water to remove the smell of the meat they have eaten. Then Liam opens the tank, and Mark throws the T-shirt over the snake's head to keep it calm. Mark picks up the snake. It twists and turns in his hands.

"You can put it down, now," Liam says, when Mark is outside.

"I can't!" Mark whispers.

"What do you mean, you can't?" says Liam.

"It's coiled around my arm!" he says, with panic rising in his voice. "Hold still," says Liam. He gently uncoils the snake until Mark is free. Then together they watch it slither off into the rainforest.

"Mission accomplished!" says Mark.

Start 2

▶ To find out what would have happened if you had started at the stepping stones, turn to page 32. ◀

New Mission

▶ To select a new mission, turn to pages 4–5. ◀

Mission Completed

▶ If you have successfully completed all three missions, turn to page 51. ◀

Start 2 | Mission: South America

Mark follows Liam across the stepping stones, to get to the far bank.

"Surely we could walk across here?" says Mark, jumping off a stone and into the water. "Look, it's not deep."

"Best not risk it," says Liam. "Piranhas are more likely to attack in shallow water, especially at this time of year."

Suddenly Mark feels something on his leg. "Piranha!" he screams.

Liam grabs Mark's arm and pulls him out. He looks him up and down.

"Panic over," he grins. "It's only a leech."

Liam removes the leech and puts it back in the water.

On the far bank, they follow the path of the river for a few miles.

"Is it much further?" asks Mark.

Liam stops to check the map but when he looks up Mark has disappeared.

He hears a whistle and runs towards the sound. Mark has fallen down the bank into some quicksand. Already the quicksand is above his knees. Mark starts to panic.

"Stay still!" calls Liam. "The more you fight it, the deeper you'll go." Liam notices that Mark's hiking pole is floating next to Mark. "Throw me your backpack," he says, "then lie back on your hiking pole."

"I'll sink!" Mark yells.

"No, you won't," says Liam. "It's easier to float in quicksand than in water. Use the pole to support your hips and let yourself float. Then pull your legs out slowly, one at a time."

It takes ages but at last Mark's legs are free and he is floating on his back in the quicksand. He inches his way towards Liam who hauls him out.

When Mark has recovered, they take the path away from the river and enter the forest. Mark is amazed by how noisy it is.

After a while, the forest opens out into a large clearing with a pool at its centre. On the far side are some huts.

"This might be a good place to stop for something to eat," says Liam. But Mark isn't listening. Above the usual forest noises, he can hear a new sound.

"What's that?" he says.

Liam stops and listens too. A loud buzzing noise is coming their way. Mark looks over his shoulder. An angry, black mass is heading straight for them.

"Killer bees!" yells Liam. "RUN!"

Mark runs towards the pool.

"Not the water!" shouts Liam.

But it's too late. Mark has already dived in.

When he comes up for air, the bees are waiting …

GAME OVER! THE KILLER BEES HAVE GOT YOU!

Start 1

▶ Turn to page 26 to restart your mission at the bridge. ◀

Survival Tip

▶ To find out how to survive an encounter with killer bees, read the extract from *Animal in Danger Safety Handbook* on page 55. ◀

New Mission

▶ To select a new mission, turn to pages 4–5. ◀

37

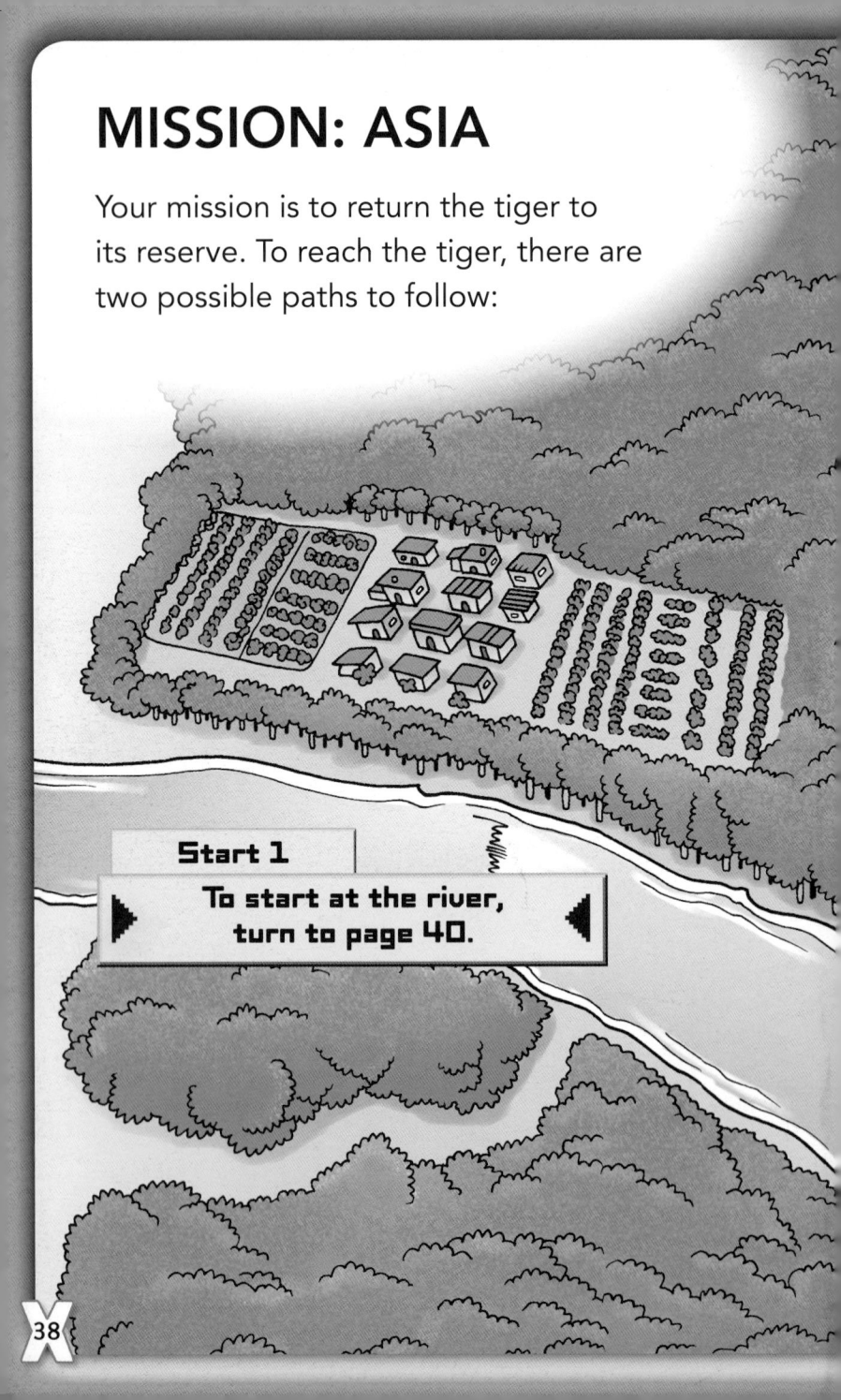

MISSION: ASIA

Your mission is to return the tiger to its reserve. To reach the tiger, there are two possible paths to follow:

Start 1

▶ **To start at the river, turn to page 40.** ◀

Start 2

▶ To start at the rocky gorge, turn to page 46. ◀

Start 1 | Mission: Asia

Liam strides down the steep path that leads to the river. Mark lags behind. He is not used to the heat and is already feeling hot and tired.

"Are we going to swim across?" he asks, as they turn a corner and see the river sparkling below them.

"What do you think?" Liam says, pointing at the river bank. Several large crocodiles are basking in the sun.

"OK, perhaps not," says Mark. "But how are we going to get to the other side?"

Liam consults the map. "There's a ferry further along the bank," he says. Mark doesn't move.

"It's not far," says Liam.

It isn't the distance that worries Mark. "What about the crocodiles?" he says.

"Didn't you read Dad's book?" asks Liam.

"Only some of it," Mark admits, sheepishly.

"OK. Keep your distance. No sudden movements and you'll be fine," Liam says.

The ferry turns out to be a small bamboo raft tethered to the bank. Liam steps on board.

"Come on. Untie the rope and hop on!" he says.

Mark hesitates. A nearby crocodile opens its jaws and shuffles forward. Mark forgets all about not making sudden movements. He yanks the rope free and leaps onto the raft. The raft dips into the water. Liam yells as he fights to keep his balance.

With a tremendous splash, Liam falls backwards into the river. One by one the crocodiles leave the bank and slip into the water.

"They're coming for Liam!" Mark thinks. "And it's all my fault!"

Mark grabs the rope and whistle from his backpack. He puts the whistle to his lips and throws one end of the rope to Liam. Mark has read the part of his dad's book that says that crocodiles have very sensitive hearing. He gives several loud blasts on the whistle as he hauls Liam back onto the raft. The crocodiles keep their distance.

Soaked and exhausted, Liam sits on the raft while Mark punts the small craft across the river.

On the other bank, the path winds its way around large rocks before it disappears into the jungle. They climb onto the rocks and rest until Liam has dried off in the sunshine.

"That was good thinking back there," Liam says, as they follow the path into the undergrowth.

Mark is pleased he has done something right at last. He is also relieved to find it is cooler under the trees.

They walk steadily for about half an hour, when Liam stops so suddenly that Mark nearly walks into him. Up ahead, a large black bear blocks their path. They both freeze.

"Put your arms out," says Liam. "Make yourself look as big as you can and back away slowly."

Mark moves backwards until he feels his back against a tree.

Mark shins up the tree. "No!" cries Liam. But it is too late. When Mark looks down, the bear is already halfway up the tree ...

GAME OVER! THE BEAR HAS GOT YOU!

Start 2
Turn to page 46 to restart your mission at the rocky gorge.

Survival Tip
To find out how to survive an encounter with a bear, read the extract from *Animals in Danger Safety Handbook* on page 56.

New Mission
To select a new mission, turn to pages 4–5.

45

Start 2 — Mission: Asia

The walls of the gorge rise steeply on both sides. Occasionally, a few rocks and pebbles roll down from the cliffs onto the ground.

"Watch out!" says Liam, as a rock comes to rest in front of Mark. "We're going to have to take care along here. The cliffs are unstable."

They walk on, scanning the rocks for movement as they go. They are about halfway into the gorge when Liam stops and kneels down. "I've got a stone in my boot," he says. "I'll catch you up."

As Mark goes ahead, he becomes aware of a rumbling sound. At first, he thinks it is thunder. But then stones and large rocks begin hurtling down the rock face, next to him.

"Landslide!" he yells.

Mark holds his backpack over his head and runs. The noise is deafening. He runs further along the gorge, dodging falling rocks and sharp stones. Then, as he leaps clear of the landslide, a rock knocks his backpack out of his hands. The bag disappears under a pile of rubble.

The noise finally stops and the dust settles. The path between Mark and his brother is totally blocked. He shouts Liam's name. From the other side of the rock pile, Liam yells back.

"I'm fine," Liam says, "but I'm going to have to go round by the other path. It's going to take me a while. I'll meet you at the village."

Mark sets off alone. As he nears the village, he sees some farmers in the distance. They are wearing masks on the back of their heads. Mark knows that a tiger will usually grab its prey by the back of the neck. The mask is there to fool the tiger and keep the farmers safe while they are working.

A farmer shows Mark where the tiger is likely to be. Taking care to stay downwind, Mark watches the tiger while he waits for Liam to arrive. He sees how thin and hungry the tiger looks. One of the tiger's legs bears the marks of a recent bad fight.

Mark is sure the tiger has wandered out of the jungle because it is injured and can no longer hunt its usual prey.

By the time Liam arrives, Mark has worked out a way to get the tiger back to the reserve. He just needs to ask the farmers for two things.

The farmers agree to give the boys some raw meat and a mask each.

With their masks in place, they lay a trail of meat from where the tiger is sleeping to the river that marks the edge of the reserve.

Later, from the safety of a tree, they watch the tiger limp along the trail, stopping to feed hungrily on the meat they have left. But when it reaches the river bank, the tiger hesitates.

"Oh no! It's not going to cross the river to the reserve!" whispers Liam.

"I know what to do," says Mark. He throws the last of the meat they have onto the far side of the river. The tiger plunges into the water.

"By the time the tiger's hungry again," says Liam, "he'll have recovered from his injury and be able to hunt in the forest."

"Mission accomplished!" says Mark.

Start 1

▶ To find out what would have happened if you had started at the river, turn to page 40. ◀

New Mission

▶ To select a new mission, turn to pages 4–5. ◀

Mission Completed

▶ If you have successfully completed all three missions, turn to page 51. ◀

Back at *Animals in Danger* headquarters, Richard is pleased to see his sons safe and sound. They look tired but well. "How did it go?" he asks.

"Mission accomplished. Or should I say, *missions* accomplished!" Liam grins.

"Well done!" Richard beams. "I'm proud of you."

"Did you have any trouble rescuing the animals?"

"No," laughs Mark. "As it turned out, rescuing the animals was the easy bit!"

"I don't understand. What do you mean?" Richard asks.

Mark and Liam exchange a look. They aren't quite sure what to say.

"Did you two get into trouble?" Richard asks, sternly.

"Nothing we couldn't handle." Liam says.

"So what happened exactly?" asks Richard.

"It's hard to know where to start," says Mark, "It's a long story."

ANIMALS IN DANGER SAFETY HANDBOOK

by Dr Richard Jones

How to survive an encounter with a baboon

What can I do to avoid them?

- Keep any food you have hidden, as baboons are known to grab food from people's hands.
- Don't look directly at a baboon or show your teeth. Baboons see this as a sign of aggression.
- Keep quiet – don't scream or wave your arms around.

What can I do if I am attacked?

- Stay calm and don't fight back unless you really have to.
- If a baboon bites you, get medical treatment as soon as you can.

How to survive an encounter with killer bees

What can I do if I am attacked?
- Run away as fast as you can and get indoors.
- Do not swat at the bees. This will just make them more aggressive.
- Do not jump into water. The bees will be waiting for you when you come out.
- Scrape any stings from your skin with your fingernail, using a sideways motion.

How to survive an encounter with a bear

What can I do to avoid them?
- Stay away from areas where bears live.
- If you need to go into an area where there might be bears, take some bear spray with you.
- In particular, keep away from bears with cubs and bears that are feeding.
- If you see a bear, make yourself look as big as possible and back away slowly and quietly.
- Do not run or climb a tree.

What can I do if I am attacked?
- Try to stay calm.
- If you are attacked, use bear spray to deter the bear.